TRAV
~ GAM

TRAVEL
~ GAMES ~

Barbara Gilgallon & Sue Seddon

WARD LOCK LIMITED · LONDON

© Text & Illustrations Ward Lock Limited 1988

First published in Great Britain in 1988
by Ward Lock Limited, 8 Clifford Street,
London W1X 1RB, an Egmont Company.

Text filmset in 10½ point Sabon
by Columns of Reading

Printed and bound in Great Britain
by William Collins Sons & Co Ltd, Glasgow

British Library Cataloguing in Publication Data

Gilgallon, Barbara
Travel games.
1. Games for travelers
I. Title   II. Seddon, Sue
790.1′922′02491   GV1206

ISBN 0–7063–6643–3

CONTENTS

Before You Go · 6
On the Lookout · 9
All Fingers & Thumbs · 17
It's Anyone's Guess · 30
Numbers Up · 37
Singalong · 42
Minds on the Move · 51
Pencil to Paper · 62
Words, Words, Words · 71
Dice & Cards · 84

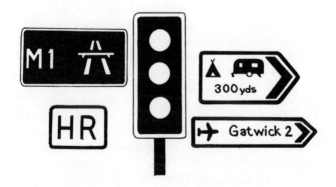

BEFORE YOU GO

So you're off on a long trip by plane, car, boat or train. The excitement of starting out can soon give way to boredom as the miles stretch ahead. The games in this book will help to pass the time and make the journey much more fun. Some of the games are designed to make you helpless with giggles, others are quieter. Some of them need equipment so before you go you'll need to collect together a few things to help you play them.

Travel Games Check List
Pack of cards; dice — two or more; calculator; pencils; paper; felt tips; face paints; string — at least 2 metres (6 ft); silver paper or foil; match box; small coins; beans, counters or other small objects; plastic cup; old magazines; paper plates; paper hankies; large paper bags; dictionary; squared paper; collection of small objects for Lucky Dip (see page 35); something large and flat to work on.

It's a good idea to put all the equipment in a box together with some wet wipes or a damp sponge in a plastic bag, some sweets (not chocolate) and some dry biscuits (for settling queasy stomachs).

Take Care Of The Driver
If you're travelling by car, you're not going to get there without the driver, so look after him or her.
- Never distract the driver. Don't tap them on the shoulder, shout suddenly in their ear, jump around in the back of the car, kick the back of the driver's seat, lean on it or grab it suddenly.
- Leave the controls to the driver, never touch them or the car keys.

- The driver's word is law and if they ask you to tone down the noise level, do it.

Take Care Of Yourself
- Fasten your seat belt.
- Keep your arms and legs inside the car.
- Never throw anything out of the window, even an apple core could cause an accident.
- Never look under the car.
- Don't use sharp objects.
- Keep heavy objects in safe places. When the car is travelling at 70 miles per hour everything in the car is moving at that speed too. If the car stops suddenly everything that isn't wearing a seat belt will keep hurtling forward, so even a can of coke can become a deadly missile.

Losing Your Lunch
Almost everyone is travel sick sometimes. It happens because of the fast movement of a car or the up and down motion of a plane or boat, when the horizon seems to leap up and down. Your eyes send confusing messages to your brain and then your stomach can't cope. If you can't take travel sickness pills there are a few things you can do to avoid feeling sick:
- Don't read.
- Don't draw or write.
- Play some quiet games to take your mind off the up and down motion of the boat or plane – get someone else to read out the rules.
- If you're in a car, open the windows – stuffy air can make you feel very sick. Don't look at the road or verge rushing by, fix your eyes on the distance, preferably through the front window.
- Ask the driver to stop before you reach the I-think-I'm-going-to-be . . . stage when it'll be too

late to reach for a paper bag anyway. Get out and
walk around for a bit.
- Going to sleep helps too, so get comfortable, relax
and start counting sheep.

That's enough do's and don'ts. One of the best
bits about going somewhere is the journey to get
there. The important thing is to enjoy your journey
wherever you're going and however you're travelling. The games in this book will help you do just
that. So if you're ready, take it steady and go!

ON THE LOOKOUT

CAR SNAP
Two or more players

Spot the matching car – each player chooses a type of car and its colour, such as a blue Renault, and then looks out for it. Call, 'Snap' when you spot a car that matches your description. You win a point if you are the first in that round. You can change the type of car from round to round or stay with the same description. It's best played for about five rounds, the winner is the player with the most number of points.

TRAVELLING ALPHABET
Two or more players

You can play this in trains and cars but you'd find it a bit difficult above the clouds or miles out to sea. The idea is to collect the complete alphabet by spotting things through the window that begin with the letters of the alphabet. They must be collected in the correct order: if you start with 'a' for antelope you can't collect 'c' for car until you've found a suitable object for 'b'. 'X' is difficult, so use objects beginning with 'ex' instead. To speed the game up you can use initial letters from road signs and advertisements. Travelling Alphabet can be played as a competition but it is more fun if everyone joins in and makes it a team effort.

RIGHT NOW
Two or more players

A spotting and guessing game. Choose an obvious object such as a bridge or a large building about a quarter of a mile ahead. Close your eyes and when you think the car has reached your chosen object, say 'Now'. If you shout early or late you can count it as a hit if you are about three cars' length from the object. No peeping! You will get more and more accurate as you play. You can take it in turns to spot objects or play the game as a competition when everyone in the car – except the driver of course – closes their eyes. The winner is the person who calls 'Now' nearest to the object.

CROSS IT OFF
Two or more players

You need to prepare this game before you set out. Make a list of twenty or so things you might see on the journey: animals, buildings, plane, train, bus, policeman, river, hill or sea. Give each player a copy of the list at the start of the game. As the player spots one of the objects on the list he or she calls it out and crosses it off the list. The other players may not cross it off their list; they have to wait for another of the same object before they can do so. It is probably best to give a time limit, say thirty minutes. The winner is the player with most objects crossed off in the time.

TRAFFIC JAM
Any number of players

Hold-ups can be really boring but you can turn them into a game if you try to guess when the traffic will move. Your car must be stationary. When you think it is about to move, say 'Traffic Jam'. Don't be tempted to shout 'Go' or your driver may drive straight into the back of the car in front. You can also play this at traffic lights which are red. Try to estimate when the lights will change to amber and say 'Change' when you think it's about to happen. When played with a lot of passengers it becomes a test of nerve to see who can hold out the longest. If you are travelling by train you can try to guess when it will leave the station. No cheating. Never hang out of the window to see if the guard is waving his flag.

MILOMETER
Two or more players

Pick an object that you think will be spotted fairly frequently while you are driving through the area. It can be a road sign, cow, crossroads, farm or church. When you've agreed on an object players guess how many of the chosen objects will be spotted as you drive a certain distance – five miles for example. State your guess out loud and beginning together count the chosen objects as a team effort. Check the distance of the milometer. At the end of five miles the winner is the player whose guess was nearest to the actual number of objects spotted.

SAFARI
Two or more players

You don't have to be travelling through the jungle to play this game. The object is to spot animals as if you are on safari. Two players or two teams of players take a different side of the road each and score points for different animals seen. The more unusual the animal, the higher the score. The scale should go something like this:

Dog	1	Goat	3
Cat	1	Donkey	4
Horse	2	Wild rabbit	4
Sheep	2	Fox	6
Cow	2	Lions, tigers, etc.	10

To make the game go faster you can include pictures of animals on advertisement hoardings and shops. The referee should set a time limit and whoever scores the most points in the time is the winner.

BEETLE DRIVE
Two or more players

You need pencil and paper and sharp eyes for this game. The object of the game is to draw a complete beetle, but you can only draw the beetle bit by bit. To start drawing you have to spot a car number plate with the number 1 in it. When you've got a number 1 you can draw the body. A number 2 on a car number plate means that you can draw the head. Each eye needs a number 3 from different number plates, each antennae a 4, also from different number plates. Find a number 5 for the tail. Just the legs left, but they are the most difficult as you must find six number 6s, all from different plates. The first player to complete a beetle calls 'Beetle' and is the winner.

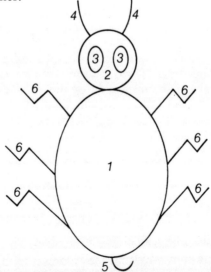

SLOGANS
Any number of players

Are you ready to giggle? Slogans is not a competitive game and it can get very silly, the sillier the better. The aim of the game is to turn the letters of number plates into slogans. For example EFP might be 'Elephant For President' or BUC might be 'Big and Ugly Club'. Don't take too long in thinking up the slogan, the faster they come out the funnier they can be. If you are uninspired by a number plate don't struggle to find a slogan, move on to the next one.

SPELLING SPOT
Any number of players

Each player writes down a word with the same number of letters, six or eight letters is about right. Then turn your sharp eyes to the passing number plates and as you spot the letters which are the same as those you've written down in your word you cross them off. To make the game more difficult take each letter from a different number plate. You can ask a referee to give you the words to begin with, but whoever chooses them, try not to include the letters Z, I, and Q as they don't appear on British number plates. The first player to cross off a complete word is the winner.

PAIRS
Two or more players

Another number plate game for two players or two teams. One side takes the number 01234 and the other the numbers 56789. To score a point you have to spot two of your numbers together in sequence on a number plate – 2, 3 or 7, 8 for example. You can also score for a double, say 5, 5 or 2, 2. The first player to score five points is the winner.

PUB SIGN TENNIS
Two players

You will see many pub signs as you travel by road. These can be turned into a game of tennis. The object is to spot as many as you can and score as you do in tennis: love, fifteen, thirty, forty, game. Two players each take a different side of the road, the front seat passenger acts as umpire. As soon as you see a pub sign and read it out you score a point; the umpire keeps the score.

TRAVELLING BINGO
Any number of players

Travelling Bingo can be played by any number of players and a caller. Each player has a card with four squares on it. In each square is a different road sign, perfectly drawn by the most artistic traveller, (or the most organized member of the party, who has managed to make the cards before setting out on the journey). Each card has different road signs on it. As road signs are passed the caller describes it and the players cross it off if they have it on their card. The first player to cross out a complete card calls 'Bingo!' and is the winner.

Travelling Bingo can be played with other objects – animals, car makes, petrol brands or a mixture of roadside or railway objects.

PAINT POTS
Two or more players

You need to know your colours to play this game. Each of the players chooses a primary colour – red, yellow or blue. The idea is to spot cars in your colour and win a point. But many cars are green, grey, brown or even orange or purple, so how do you score points for spotting those? Well, all these colours can be mixed from primary colours:

yellow + blue = green
red + yellow = orange
red + blue = purple
blue + red + yellow = brown or grey

If a green car is spotted yellow and blue players can try for it. The first one to say 'green' wins the point and so on. White contains all the colours so everyone gets a point. Black cars don't count because black does not contain colour. Two-tone cars are a free for all, the first player to say the colour gets a point.

ALL ABROAD
Any number of players

Cars travelling abroad usually have signs on them which identify their country of origin. British cars have GB for example. It's fascinating to see how many countries you can identify. The list below gives the most common ones.

A	Austria	IRL	Republic of Ireland
AUS	Australia		
B	Belgium	L	Luxembourg
CAN	Canada	N	Norway
CH	Switzerland	NL	Netherlands
CS	Czechoslovakia	NZ	New Zealand
CY	Cyprus	P	Portugal
D	Germany	PL	Poland
DK	Denmark	R	Romania
E	Spain	S	Sweden
F	France	SU	Russia
GR	Greece	USA	United States of America
H	Hungary		
I	Italy	YU	Yugoslavia

MAKE UP A STORY
Any number of players

If you've had enough of spotting and competitive games it's good fun to make up stories about people in passing cars or trains. What are their names? are they going? What will they do when they get there? The funnier the story you make up the better. It's not a good idea to make up stories about fellow passengers on a train or plane, they might take offence!

TRAVELLING CONSEQUENCES
Two or more players

You need your memory and a sense of the ridiculous for this game. One player spots something out of the window, for example a woman with an umbrella, and says, 'Did you see that woman with an umbrella walking along?' The next player repeats the sentence and adds what he or she has seen: 'Did you see that woman with the umbrella walking along with a chimpanzee in a cage?' Take it in turns to add to the list, (which can become quite hilarious). You must repeat it correctly which gets more and more difficult. If you get the list wrong you can have a second attempt. If you still get it wrong, you have to drop out. It's more fun with several players but it's quite possible to play with two. To avoid arguments it's quite a good idea to have someone to act as a judge. The winner is the last person left in.

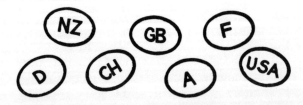

ALL FINGERS & THUMBS

FINGER CHALLENGES
Any number of players

Can you:
1 Make your little finger and index finger meet? If you can, can you bring your middle two fingers up through the gap?
2 Bend your hand and touch your wrist with your thumb?
3 Separate your first and second fingers from your third and fourth fingers, keeping them in pairs and repeat it very quickly?
4 Bend your index finger at the middle joint whilst keeping the top two sections straight?

BODY CHALLENGES
Any number of players

Can you:
1 Rub your tummy whilst patting your head?
2 Touch the end of your nose with your tongue?
3 Touch your nose with your right hand and at the same time your right ear with your left hand, clap your hands in front then touch your nose with your left hand and your left ear with your right hand? How fast can you keep this going?

HOLE IN THE HAND
One player

You can even fool yourself with this little trick. Roll a thin magazine or newspaper into a tube about 2.5 cm (1 in) in diameter. Hold it up to your right eye. You should be able to see all the way down. Now bring your left hand up to within a few centimetres of your left eye, palm facing you, little finger resting on the tube. Close both eyes, then open them. You should be able to see a hole in your hand.

THE FLOATING SAUSAGE
One player

Here's another trick which makes you see things which aren't there. Make your hands into fists, stretch out your index fingers and make the tips touch. Then bring your hands up to about 20 cm (8 in) in front of your nose and look at the place where they join, then look through them. As you do so draw your fingers slightly apart and look through the gap, focusing your eyes on the far side of the space in which you are sitting. A floating sausage will appear in front of your eyes.

THE FORCE IS WITH YOU
One or more players

Make each of your hands into a fist and put them together so that your fingers meet at the second joint. Raise your third fingers to make a spire, the fingers should join at the top. Make sure that the rest of the joints are still touching tightly. Now try to separate the tips of your third fingers without separating your joints. However hard you try, the knuckles separate when the tips of your spire part. Challenge your fellow travellers and see if they can achieve the impossible.

SCISSORS, PAPER, STONE
Two or three players

This game has been played all round the world for centuries and is still very popular.

Each player puts one hand behind his or her back. On the count of three you bring out your hidden hand as scissors, paper or stone.

Scissors Two fingers extended.
Paper All fingers and thumb extended.
Stone Hand in a fist.

If there are two of you playing and both of you show the same sign then no points are scored because it's a draw, but if you show different signs this is how to score:

Scissors score over paper because they can cut it.
Paper scores over stone because it can wrap it.
Stone scores over scissors because it can blunt them.

The winner of the round scores a point.

It's possible to play this game with three people. If all three show a different sign no one scores because the signs cancel each other out. If two players show stone and you show scissors they get a point each and you score nothing. If they show paper and you show scissors you score two points and they score nothing.

ODD OR EVEN
Two or more players

Odd or Even is similar to Scissors, Paper, Stone, but the object is to guess whether your opponent will show an odd or even number of fingers. Toss a coin to see who will be first caller.

On the word go, players tap their fists on their knees twice as if knocking on a door. Instead of making a third knock they open out one or two fingers and the caller has to call 'Odd' or 'Even' just before the fingers open. If the caller guesses correctly he or she gets one point and another go as caller, get it wrong and you score nothing and the other player becomes caller on the next round.

If there are three players try Odd Man Out: on

the third knock show either one or two fingers, you
don't have to shout 'Odd' or 'Even', the person who
shows a different number of fingers is the 'odd man'
and the other two score a point each.

CALL OF THE WILD
Two to four players

Call Of The Wild is another version of Odd and
Even. You can play with two, three or four players.
Each player chooses an animal and imitates its call.
Short simple sounds are best such as the grunt of a
pig, the bark of a dog or the roar of a lion. To play
the game you must remember everyone's call. On
'Go' everyone taps their knees with their hands three
times. On the fourth go they open out one, two or
three fingers. If two players show the same number
of fingers they try to be the first to make the other
player's animal call. If they get it right they score a
point. As you can imagine, it can get quite noisy, so
choose your time to play it carefully, but it's
guaranteed to have you helpless with laughter.

FINGER PUPPETS
One or more players

If you draw tiny faces on the tips of your fingers
with washable felt tip pen you can make finger
puppets. You can put on a complete play because
you'll have as many as ten characters to act in it.

Paper tissues make good costumes – cloaks,
scarves and hats are easiest.

ONE POTATO
Two or more players

This is a counting out game for as many players as
you like. Each player makes his or her hands into
fists or potatoes and holds them out in front. Take it
in turn to be the counter.

One potato, two potatoes,
Three potatoes, four,
Five potatoes, six potatoes,
Seven potatoes more.

As you say each number in the rhyme the counter taps each player's potatoes in turn, including his or her own. When you say the word 'more' the potato being tapped must be taken away. Start the rhyme again and go on until there is only one potato left. The last potato in is the winner.

WELL BALANCED
One or more players
It's quite a challenge to see if you can balance a small object somewhere on your person while the car, train, plane or boat is rolling along. A ball of screwed up paper is ideal but you could use a coin or a match box. Issue a challenge to your other passengers and see how long they can balance a small ball of paper on their knee or palm or elbow or finger. Do not issue dangerous challenges – you forfeit a go if you do. The winner is the player whose balancing act lasts the longest and he or she issues the next challenge.

TORN JIGSAW
Two players (or more if there's room)
If you have an old magazine with you tear out a full page picture each. Do not show it to the other player and do not tear pages out of magazines people are reading, it tends to make them very cross. Each player tears his or her picture into small shapes about 3 cm (1¼ in) across. Place them all, right side up but well shuffled, on a flat surface and challenge your partner to fit the jigsaw together. The first one to complete the picture is the winner.

CAT'S CRADLE
Two or more players

Cat's Cradle is a traditional game played with a piece of string tied in a loop.

You need a piece of string about 1½–2 metres (5–6 ft) long, tied in a loop. The basic idea is to weave shapes with the loop of string across the hands. Your partner then picks up the string, transfers it to his or her hands making a new pattern as the string changes hands.

Naming the parts:
Thumb
Index finger Next to the thumb
Middle finger The long one next to the index finger
Third finger Next to the middle finger
Little finger
Palm string Any string that goes across your palm.

How to play
First player: Hold your hands out in front of you, fingers pointing upwards, palms facing each other, the loop of string around your hands as shown in the drawing.

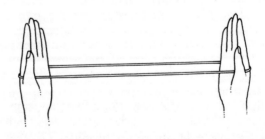

Pass your right hand under the string near your left hand and return your hand to the starting position, repeat the action with your left hand. You should now have a loop of string around each palm.

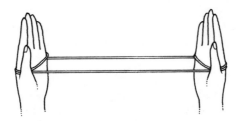

Slip the middle finger of your right hand under the palm string of your left hand. Draw your right hand back to the starting position. Slip the middle finger of your left hand under the palm string of your right hand and draw your hand back to the starting position. It should look like this:

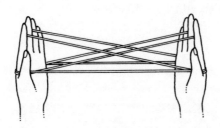

If it does, well done, you have made *The Cat's Cradle.*

Second player: Look carefully at the Cat's Cradle. You will see that the strings cross in two places. Use your thumb and index finger and grip the crossed strings and pull them apart.

Pull your fingers down and take the crossed strings under the parallel strings and up through the middle of them. Stretch out your index fingers and thumbs. This will take up the slack in the string and you will be holding the string yourself.

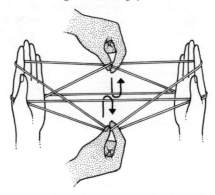

First player: Gently extricate your hands and let your partner take over the pattern. It's called *The Bed* and should look like this:

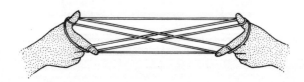

First player: Using your index fingers and thumbs take hold of the crossed strings and pull them apart, then duck them under the parallel strings and bring them up through the middle. If you stretch out the fingers holding the string you will take over the pattern and your partner can withdraw his or her hands gently. Well done, you have now made *The Two Candles* and it looks like this:

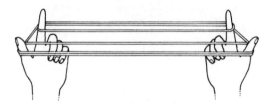

Second player: Hook your little fingers under the opposite centre strings and pull them apart over the outside strings like this:

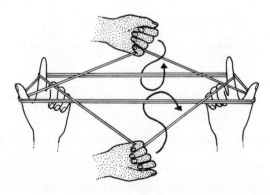

Hang on to them while you duck your index finger and thumb under the outside strings and bring them up through the middle. Stretch out your fingers and take the strain of the pattern.

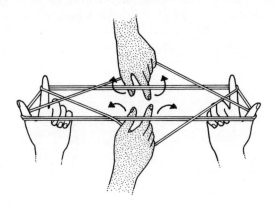

First player: Gently let go and remove your hands. You have now made *The Manger* and it should look like this:

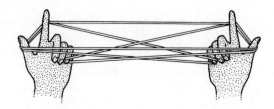

First player: Grip the crossed strings with your index fingers and thumbs and pull them out, then up and over the outside of the parallel strings and down into the centre of the pattern. Stretch out and take over, your partner can release his or her hands.

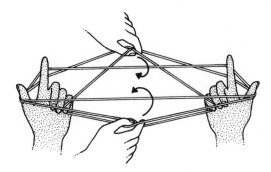

You have now made the *Saint Andrew's Cross* and your pattern should now look like this:

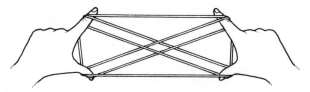

FINGER RHYMES FOR SMALL PEOPLE

Toddlers enjoy rhymes with finger play. Here are some favourites:

Here Is The Church

Here is the church,
(Interlock your hands knuckles on top, fingers bent down inside, thumbs together to form the doors.)
Here is the steeple,
(Raise your index fingers, tips touching to form a steeple.)
Open the doors
(Part your thumbs.)
And here are the people.
(Keeping your fingers interlaced, turn your hands over and wiggle your fingers.)

Here is the minister
Going upstairs,
   *(Separate your hands and walk the fingers of your
   right hand across the fingers of your left (which
   should be palm up).)*
He's up in the pulpit
   *(Cross your wrists and clasp your hands down in
   front of you, twist your clasped hands up between
   your arms.)*
Saying his prayers.
   (Wiggle a thumb above your clasped hands.

I'm A Little Teapot
Small children can manage these actions quite easily.

I'm a little tea pot
Short and stout.
   (Say the first two lines without actions.)
Here's my handle.
   (Right hand on hip elbow bent to form handle.)
Here's my spout.
   *(Hold left arm up bent at elbow and wrist to form
   spout.)*
When I get my steam up
Hear me shout,
   (Whistle or puff at end of line.)
Tip me up
And pour me out.
   *(Keeping teapot shape bend to the left at the waist
   as if pouring out a cup of tea.)*

Two Little Dicky Birds
   Two little dicky birds sitting on a wall,
   One named Peter, one named Paul.
   Fly away Peter, fly away Paul,
   Come back Peter, come back Paul.

As you say the first line, rest the middle finger of each hand on a table, the back of a car seat or your lap. On the words 'Peter' and 'Paul' in the second line, lift one of the fingers for each name. As you say the names in the third line, fold each finger down so that they disappear, and put them back again as you say the fourth line.

Round And Round The Garden

Round and round the garden, like a teddy bear,
One step, two step and tickle you under there.

Trace your finger round on the palm of the baby's hand as you say the first line. As you say 'One step' walk your finger onto the wrist, as you say 'Two step' walk it to the elbow and tickle the baby under the arm as you say 'Tickle you under there'.

MONEY BOX
Two or more players

You need a small box for this game. An empty match box is ideal but an empty cigarette packet will do. Without showing the other players, the challenger puts some coins into the box and then challenges the others to guess how much is in the money box. They are allowed to feel its weight and to rattle it but, of course, they mustn't open it. The player who guesses closest to the actual amount wins the round and becomes the challenger for the next round.

Money box can also be played by asking an adult to act as challenger for every round. When you play this version the winner gets a small prize – one or two coins from the box – and the challenger inserts a new amount for the next round.

SHOPPER FROM OUTER SPACE
Two or more players

In this game, an alien from outer space has landed on Earth and goes shopping. One player acts as the alien and the other players are the shop assistants. They can't speak the alien's language and it can't speak theirs, but the creature from outer space is desperate to buy something. The only way it can make shop assistants understand is to mime the object that it wants to buy. The shop assistants have to guess what it wants.

The alien decides what it wants to buy and mimes it to the other players. The shop assistant who manages to guess the object becomes the alien in the next round.

I-SPY
Two or more players

Everyone knows the rules of I-Spy but in case you've forgotten here they are again:

One player sees an object and says 'I spy with my little eye something beginning with . . .' and says the initial letter of the object he or she has chosen. The other players then have to guess what it is. Whoever guesses picks the next object.

When you are travelling at speed 'I-Spy' can be tricky, as the object may be miles behind you before anyone has had a chance to guess. It helps if you choose something in the distance ahead of you. Alternatively you can pick something in or on the car such as a windscreen wiper. If you are playing in a train, ship or plane then you must pick something that is easily visible all the time, not the airport you have just left behind!

COLOUR I-SPY
Two or more players (good for the very young)

You play this game in a similar way to original I-Spy but instead of giving an object's initial letter you give its colour. 'I spy with my little eye something that is red', or green or blue, etc. It's a good game to play with very young children who may not know the initial letter of an object but will certainly know its colour. Don't pick something that will disappear in a flash as you cruise down the motorway, it's unfair on the guessers.

BOTTICELLI
Two or more players

Botticelli is quite a challenge so it's best played by older children. Younger ones will manage it if the characters they have to guess are very well known to them.

The challenger chooses a famous person, dead or alive, fact or fiction. All he tells the rest of the players about the character is the first letter of the name by which the character is best-known. The rest of the players have to guess the identity of the character but they have to do so in a particular way. They must think of a famous character and ask their question using clues about the character so that the challenger also has to guess who they mean. If he can't the other player gets a free go and can ask a direct question. It all goes something like this:

Challenger: 'My name begins with M.'
Questioner: 'Are you a blonde film star who died young?'
Challenger: 'No I'm not Marilyn Monroe.'
Questioner: 'Are you a brilliant South American footballer?'
Challenger: 'No I'm not Maradonna.'
Questioner: 'Did you invent the bicycle?'
Challenger: 'I don't know who invented the bicycle.'
Questioner: 'It was Macmillan. I get a free go. Are you an animal?'
Challenger: 'Yes.'
Questioner: 'Are you a mouse that wears red trousers and has a girlfriend called Minnie?'
Challenger: 'Yes, I am Mickey Mouse.'

WHO AM I
Two or more players

This is a less complicated game than Botticelli so it can be played with younger children. One person is the challenger and thinks of a famous person, again fact or fiction, historical or modern. The questioners ask simple questions such as 'Are you a man?' or

'Are you alive?' It's best to limit the number of questions to twenty. If the questioners can't guess then the challenger gets another go. The player who guesses the character becomes the challenger. If the challenger picks a very obscure character he or she is disqualified and another is chosen.

ANIMAL, VEGETABLE AND MINERAL
Two or more players

Players in this game try to guess the object rather than a person. The challenger thinks of an object and then gives the other players a clue by telling them whether the object is animal, vegetable or mineral. Animals are easy – a dog is obviously an animal. Vegetable is used to describe anything that grows or once grew such as a tree or a wooden table but a plastic table is mineral. Some objects need descriptions – a pencil is vegetable and mineral because it is made of wood and graphite. The challenger can only answer yes or no to questions. Limit the questions to twenty or the game will go on for too long and everyone will become bored.

HEADS AND TAILS
Two players

Spinning a coin is usually used to make a decision but it also makes a good guessing game. Players have to guess whether the coin will come up heads or tails. It's more fun if the coin becomes a prize as well, so if you don't want it to bankrupt the family have a bag of pennies ready for this game.

COFFEEPOT
Two or more players

If you've never played Coffeepot you've missed a lot of fun. You can manage with two players but it's best played with three, four or more.

One player puts his hands over his or her ears so that the others can choose a word without being overheard. The word can be a noun or a verb and it's even better if it's both. The guesser then has to find out what the word is by asking questions. The players answer in sentences in which they must use the word but they never say the actual word, they use 'coffeepot' instead. It goes like this:

Guesser: 'Is our journey going to be very long?'
Player: 'Yes, I'm going to coffeepot the road very carefully.'
Guesser: 'Will we see some interesting things on the way?'
Player: 'I expect so, we could coffeepot out for the sea.'
Guesser: 'What time will we get there?'
Player: 'I'm not sure, I'll look at my coffeepot and tell you.'
Guesser: 'Got it! It's watch isn't it?'

HIDE AND SEEK
Two or more players

Yes, you can play hide and seek while strapped into your seat belt whether you are on a plane or in a car! But you do need a lot of imagination because you hide in your mind. One player chooses a place to hide and imagines he or she is there. It could be under your bed at home. It could be in the cottage where you've just spent your holiday or in a wood or castle that you've visited. The other players try to guess where you are hidden. They've only got twenty questions so getting the right place in the right building or wood is near enough. It's a bit much to expect them to guess that you are on the second branch in the fifth tree from the stile in the wood near the village. The hider can give clues by saying warm or cold depending on whether the players are getting near the hiding place. The player who makes the nearest guess takes the next turn to 'hide'.

LIP READING
Two or more players

Lip reading is quite a skill and takes a lot of practice but you can make quite a game of it and learn a new skill at the same time. You can think up an interesting sentence or use a well known phrase or saying such as 'A rolling stone gathers no moss'. If you are playing with young children mouth the first line of a nursery rhyme. Mouth the words very clearly to the other players. The player who guesses the whole phrase takes the next turn to think of a sentence.

GUESS THE SOUND
Two or more players

You need to be quite inventive to play this. You may have to make the sound of someone getting up in the morning, going downstairs, pouring cereal into a bowl, washing it up and then cleaning teeth and getting dressed. One players tells a simple story but substitutes sounds for actions. The other players have to guess what he or she is doing from the sounds. Make the stories short and simple and funny if you can. Take it in turns to tell the story.

LUCKY DIP
Two or more players

There won't actually be a proper bran-tub on your journey but you can prepare a large bag full of objects and get the players to feel them through the bag and try to guess what they are. If you are really organized they could be wrapped which makes the guessing more difficult and more fun. The contents could be a great assortment ranging from keys and cassettes to things that the players can eat if they guess correctly, such as crisps or sweets, or a small car to play with or a felt tip. It's a good game to keep until that awful moment when everyone starts asking 'How much further?'

WHAT A WHOPPER!
Two or more players

Only one player, the commentator, keeps his eyes open in this game so don't encourage the driver to play. Ready? Close your eyes. The commentator describes what is on the road and at the side as it passes by. The other players have to guess whether it's a car, a lorry, a shop, a farm and so on. Sounds easy? Well it isn't because the commentator throws in a few whoppers just to confuse everyone. He might describe a fair or a castle. They won't actually be there of course, so as well as guessing what each object is the other players have to say whether it's true or false too.

If the commentator is clever he can fool the players into thinking that real objects are false and false objects are real.

Don't commentate for too long or the game becomes boring. Limit commentary time to two or three minutes and award points each time a player is wrong. The player with the least points is the winner.

EGG AND BACON

This is a great game for those who need to learn their tables. Any two numbers from 0 to 9 are chosen. Supposing they are 2, and 7. Everyone has to count to a chosen number, say 30. Now comes the difficult bit. Every time you come to a multiple of 2 you must say 'Eggs' and for every multiple of 7 you must say 'Bacon'. The sequence for these numbers would sould like this:

1, 'Eggs', 3, 'Eggs', 5, 'Eggs', 'Bacon', 'Eggs',
9, 'Eggs', 11 'Eggs', 13, 'Eggs and Bacon'.

The last number in this sequence (14) is a multiple of both numbers and so the players have to say 'Eggs' *and* 'Bacon'. You can play this all together for fun or individually with the other players challenging you if they think that you have missed a number.

NUMBER PLATE BINGO
Two or more players

Before play begins each player compiles a Bingo card. Everyone selects their own set of ten two-digit numbers. The set of numbers may look like this:

	42		57		16	
22		85		39		97
	12		58		26	

Now the players have to keep a lookout to find these numbers on the number plates of passing cars. The number may be part of a longer number e.g. ABC 716 or ASD 970.

The first player to find all the numbers on their card is the winner.

If there are not many cars on the road it can take rather a long time to get a 'full house'. If this is the case it is a good idea to set a time limit and see who has the most numbers crossed off at the end. Do remember to call out 'Bingo' as quietly as you can as it can give everyone quite a start – including the driver.

REVERSED RESULT

This trick with numbers will really make your friends feel that you can read their minds. When no one is looking write the number 1089 on a piece of paper and put it in your pocket. Now ask one of your fellow travellers to write down any number with three digits – as long as they are in descending order e.g. 541. You then ask them to reverse the number e.g. 145. Ask them to take the second number from the first $541 - 145 = 396$. Your friend must then add the reverse of this number $396 + 693 = 1089$. With a grand flourish you now produce the paper from your pocket and announce that you knew the number that they would arrive at. As long as the trick is done in the correct sequence the number will always be 1089.

LICENCE TO COUNT

There are two ways to play this game, the second a little harder than the first. Start with the first and go on to the other.

Two players or two teams look out for number plates which end in the numbers 0 to 9. The first one to collect a set of numbers in the correct order is the winner.

The harder version of this is basically the same idea but all the numbers have to be collected in sequence:

ABC *101*
EKG *124*
BHF *823*

The last number collected should be one that includes 89.

GET CALCULATING

You may not have realized it but your calculator can speak. Well, write messages, anyway. Try this one for starters. Multipy 7 by 2 and turn your calculator upside down to find a greeting. There are many other words which appear when you tap in the right calculation. Now try these:

616 × 5	A musical instrument
5864 ÷ 8	A slippery fish
2754267 × 2	Is this what teachers say about the headmaster?
15470 − 1 × 5	Found on the beach
1000 − 899 × 5	Help!
19246 × 3	Heard on Sundays
591069 − 55555	Sound made by a reptile
99^2 − 2087	Where Jack and Jill descended
2517 + 1234	Wight, Man or Aran?
4213 × 11 + 11375	Unwelcome post
2000 + 101 × 18	The vicar's favourite book?

NUMBER MAGIC

You can pretend that you have been mind reading when you perform this trick. First of all ask a fellow passenger to think of a number between 1 and 50. They write this number down and put it in their pocket. They then choose a number between 50 and 100 and write this down on a piece of paper too. Now ask your friend to take away the first number from 99 and to add the result to the second number. Now they must cross off the first digit from the new number and add one to the result. Finally the second number is subtracted from the original one. Ask your friend what the new number is. They should find that it is the same as the number in their pocket.

CONNECT THE NUMBER

This game will really make you think. The players take it in turns to call out a number betwen 1 and 12. The next player has to think of something associated with that number. For example if the number is 3 you could say, 'Three Blind Mice' or 'Triangle' or 'Three French Hens' (from the Christmas song). After the first round you are not allowed to repeat an association which has been used before. If a player cannot think of a connection it passes to the next and they may earn the point. The game can go on until everyone has exhausted their store of numbers. The driver or a non-player may need to referee if a connection is disputed.

TIMES UP

Are you the sort of person who loses track of time? This game will sharpen up your timekeeping. One person keeps an eye on a clock or watch and all the players have to guess the time it takes to travel a certain number of miles. This could be anything up to ten. When each player has had a guess the timekeeper shouts, 'Go!'. At the end of the distance the nearest guess to the correct time is the winner. On a train or a bus you could try to guess the time between stops.

TIME FLIES

This is a variation on Times Up. This time everybody has to try to guess when five minutes have passed. This is actually quite difficult. If a player feels that five minutes have passed since the starting signal they call 'Now'. The clockwatcher tells them if they are correct or not. If someone manages to guess exactly, the game is over right away. Otherwise the nearest guess to five minutes is the winner.

ROWS OF TWELVE

This is a number challenge that you can try to work out on your own or in a race with a friend. Seven circles are drawn, three at the top, three at the bottom and one in the middle. The problem is to place the number 1–7 in such a way that the joining rows all add up to twelve.

Solution:

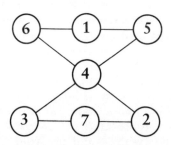

SAINTS AND SINNERS
Two or more players

In this game one team is known as the Saints and the other the Sinners. Once the terms have been sorted out you set to work looking for number plates. When one has been spotted both teams quickly add up the numbers. If the result is under 13 it is a point to the Saints. If over 13 the Sinners collect the point. A total of 13 exactly gives both teams a point. This can be played with a time limit or for the duration of the journey.

SINGALONG

Singing on a journey is a marvellous way to make the time pass enjoyably but unless you're in a private jet or you've hired a train for a day, it's best confined to car travellers, as other passengers may take a very dim view of your musical offerings.

The songs included in this section are traditional old favourites. If you are not sure of some of the tunes, someone travelling with you is bound to know at least one of them so that you will have learned a new song by the end of the journey. Several of the songs are designed to stretch your memory as you have to repeat phrases or verses, which can become quite a challenge. Always remember that the driver's word is law, so if he or she asks you to shut up, do!

NAME THAT TUNE

It can be really infuriating if someone insists on singing when you want to be quiet but if you gently tap the rhythm of a tune you can turn it into a game. Tap out easy tunes at first – nursery rhymes are good to begin with – and get your partner(s) to guess the tune. The person who names the tune taps out the next mystery melody. It's a good game if you're somewhere like a plane or train where singing out loud is guaranteed to drive other passengers wild.

GUESS THE JINGLE

A car or other form of private transport is best for this one. La or hum the tune of a well-known TV jingle and get everyone to guess the advert. The person who guesses correctly has the next go.

SONGS
She'll Be Coming Round The Mountain
1 She'll be coming round the mountain when she
   comes
   She'll be coming round the mountain when she
   comes,
   She'll be coming round the mountain,
   Coming round the mountain,
   She'll be coming round the mountain when she
   comes.

Chorus
   Singing yi, yi, yippee, yippee, yi,
   Singing yi, yi, yippee, yippee, yi
   Singing, yi, yi, yippee, yi, yi, yippee,
   Yi, yi, yippee, yippee, yi.

2 She'll be driving six white horses when she comes
3 Oh we'll all go out to meet her when she comes
4 We will kill the old red rooster when she comes
5 And we'll all have chicken and dumplings when
   she comes

Old MacDonald Had A Farm
1 Old MacDonald had a farm, E, I, E, I, O
   And on this farm he had some chicks, E, I, E, I, O
   With a chick, chick here and a chick, chick there,
   Here a chick, there a chick, everywhere a chick,
   chick.
   Old MacDonald had a farm, E, I, E, I, O.

Repeat with:
2 Turkeys – gobble, gobble
3 Pigs – grunt, grunt
4 Sheep – baa, baa
5 Cows – moo, moo

You can go on adding until you can't stand it any
more!

Ten Green Bottles

1 Ten green bottles standing on a wall,
  Ten green bottles standing on a wall,
  And if one green bottle should accidentally fall,
  There'd be nine green bottles standing on the wall.

2 Nine green bottles standing on a wall,
  Nine green bottles standing on a wall

  And so on until there is:
  One green bottle standing on the wall,
  One green bottle standing on a wall,
  And if one green bottle should accidentally fall,
  There'd be no green bottles standing on the wall.

Ten In The Bed

There were ten in the bed and the little one said,
Roll over, roll over.
So they all rolled over and one fell out,
There were nine in the bed and the little one said,
Roll over, roll over.
So they all rolled over and one fell out,
There were eight in the bed and the little one said,
Roll over, roll over.

Continue until there is no-one left in the bed.

John Brown's Baby
Sung to the tune of John Brown's Body.

1 John Brown's baby has a cold upon its chest,
  John Brown's baby has a cold upon its chest,
  John Brown's baby has a cold upon its chest
  So we rubbed it with camphorated oil.

Chorus
  Camphor, camphor, camphor-a-ted,
  Camphor, camphor, camphor-a-ted,
  Camphor, camphor, camphor-a-ted,
  So we rubbed it with camphorated oil.

2 Sing a second time but don't sing the word 'baby',
  mime rocking one instead.
3 Sing a third time, don't sing 'baby' and don't sing
  'cold' – cough instead.
4 Sing a fourth time leaving out 'baby', 'cold' and
  'rubbed' – mime rubbing chest instead.
5 Sing a fifth time holding noses instead of singing
  'camphorated oil'.

The chorus is sung in full between each verse.

London Bridge

1 London Bridge is falling down,
  Falling down, falling down.
  London Bridge is falling down,
  My fair lady.

2 Build it up with iron bars,
  Iron bars, iron bars.
  Build it up with iron bars,
  My fair lady.

3 Iron bars will rust away,
4 Build it up with pins and needles,
5 Pins and needles will rust and bend,
6 Build it up with penny loaves,
7 Penny loaves will tumble down,
8 Build it up with gold and silver,
9 Gold and silver I have not got,

10 London Bridge is falling down,
   Falling down, falling down.
   London Bridge is falling down,
   My fair lady.

One Men Went To Mow

1 One man went to mow,
   Went to mow a meadow,
   One man and his dog
   Went to mow a meadow.

2 Two men went to mow,
   Went to mow a meadow,
   Two men, one man and his dog
   Went to mow a meadow.

3 Three men went to mow,
   Went to mow a meadow,
   Three men, two men, one man and his dog
   Went to mow a meadow.

And so on until your patience runs out.

Bobby Shafto

1 Bobby Shafto's gone to sea,
   Silver buckles on his knee.
   He'll come back and marry me,
   Bonny Bobby Shafto.

2 Bobby Shafto's young and fair,
   Combing down his yellow hair.
   He's my love for evermore
   Bonny Bobby Shafto.

Row, Row, Row Your Boat (A Round)

   Row, row, row your boat
   Row, row, row, your boat,
   Gently down the stream,
   Merrily, merrily, merrily, merrily,
   Life is but a dream.

London's Burning (A Round)
London's burning, London's burning,
Fetch the engine, fetch the engine,
Fire, fire! Fire, fire!
Pour on water, pour on water.

A round is a song where everyone sings the same tune but each singer starts at a different time. In 'London's Burning' the first singer starts and sings the first line alone and then continues to the end of the song. The second singer begins the first line as soon as the first singer begins the second line and so on. It's quite possible for two singers to sing the round but it sounds even better if four singers take part. Whoever comes in last will sing the last line alone. Before you begin to sing a round make sure that everyone knows the tune very well because it can be quite difficult to keep your part while everyone else is singing theirs.

If You're Happy
This is a traditional American song and should be sung with all the actions.

1 If you're happy and you know it
   Clap your hands, (clap, clap)
   If you're happy and you know it
   Clap your hands, (clap, clap)
   If you're happy and you know it
   Then you'll surely want to show it
   If you're happy and you know it,
   Clap your hands. (clap, clap)

2 If you're happy and you know it
   Click your fingers,

3 If you're happy and you know it
   Slap your sides,

4 If you're happy and you know it
Stamp your feet,

5 If you're happy and you know it
Shout 'We are'

6 If you're happy and you know it
Do all five,

Michael Finnagen
Chorus
There was an old man named Michael Finnagen,
He grew whiskers on his chinagen,
The wind came up and blew them inagen.
Poor old Michael Finnagen, beginagen.

1 There was an old man named Michael Finnagen,
He got drunk through drinking ginagen,
Thus he wasted all his tinagen.

2 There was an old man named Michael Finnagen,
He kicked up an awful dinagen,
Because they said he must not sinagen.

3 There was an old man named Michael Finnagen,
He went fishing with a pinagen,
Caught a fish and dropped it inagen.

4 There was an old man named Michael Finnagen,
Climed a tree and barked his shinagen,
Took off several yards of skinagen.

5 There was an old man named Michael Finnagen,
He grew fat and then grew thinagen,
Then he died and had to beginagen.
Poor old Michael Finnagen, beginagen.

What Shall We Do With The Drunken Sailor?

1 What shall we do with the drunken sailor,
   What shall we do with the drunken sailor,
   What shall we do with the drunken sailor,
   Early in the morning?

Chorus
   Hooray and up she rises,
   Hooray and up she rises,
   Hooray and up she rises,
   Early in the morning.

2 Put him in the long boat until he's sober,
3 Pull out the plug and wet him all over,
4 Put him in the scuppers with the hose pipe on
   him,
5 Heave him by the leg in a running bowlin',
6 Tie him to the taffrail when she's yard-arm under,

I Know An Old Lady Who Swallowed a Fly

1 I know an old lady who swallowed a fly
   I don't know why she swallowed a fly,
   Perhaps she'll die.

2 I know an old lady who swallowed a spider
   That wriggled and jiggled and tickled inside her.
   She swallowed the spider to catch the fly
   I don't know why she swallowed the fly,
   Perhaps she'll die.

3 I know an old lady who swallowed a bird,
   How absurd to swallow a bird.
   She swallowed the bird the catch the spider,
   She swallowed the spider to catch the fly,
   I don't know why she swallowed the fly.
   Perhaps she'll die.

4 I know an old lady who swallowed a cat.
   Imagine that! She swallowed a cat.

She swallowed the cat to catch the bird . . . ,
(Plus spider, plus fly)

5 I know an old lady who swallowed a dog,
What a hog to swallow a dog!
She swallowed the dog to catch the cat . . .
(Plus bird, plus spider, plus fly)

6 I know an old lady who swallowed a goat,
Opened her throat and swallowed a goat.
She swallowed the goat to catch the dog,
(Plus cat, plus bird, plus spider, plus fly)

7 I know an old lady who swallowed a cow,
I don't know how she swallowed a cow.
She swallowed the cow to catch the goat . . .
(Plus dog, plus cat, plus bird, plus spider, plus fly)

8 I know an old lady who swallowed a horse
She's dead of course.

MINDS ON THE MOVE

NAME A HOBBY

This is an amusing game for any number of travellers. Each person takes their own initials and makes up a hobby which begins with those letters. The next stage is to make a list of family, friends and classmates and invent weird and wonderful hobbies for them as well.

Supposing that your list included the following: John Thorn, Arthur Furwell and Clare Green. Their hobbies could be – Juggling Tadpoles, Acting Foolishly and Collecting Gobstoppers.

The idea is to make your list as daft as possible. You could either make up the hobbies as a group effort or write down individual lists. These could be compared at the end and a point given to the person with the best hobby for each name. To speed the game up, set a time limit.

LIST BUILDING

This list game is played against the clock. Each player has one minute to list as many items as he or she can within a given category. Ten different categories are written on pieces of paper and the player picks out one of them. These should be fairly wide and might include sports, food, animals, hobbies, countries, items of clothing, parts of the body, etc.

At a signal the players lists as many objects in his category as possible. This may be written down but it is more fun to do it out loud. The other players keep count and the score is added up at the end of one minute. The player with the greatest number of items in his or her list is the winner.

QUESTIONS, QUESTIONS

This game is best played with two players.

The idea is to carry on a conversation using nothing but questions. The first player to make a statement rather than ask a question is out. The conversation might go like this:

'Are you happy?'
'What about?'
'Can't you guess?'
'How should I know?'
'Know about what?'
'What did you say?'
'Didn't you hear me?'
'Can't you speak louder?'
'Of course I can!'

The last comment is a statement and so the player is out. If you wanted to make the game longer the winner could score one point. The first player to collect five points would be the winner. A player can be challenged if his or her sentence does not appear to make sense or have nothing to do with the previous question. Repetition can also be challenged.

KIM'S GAME

How good is your memory?

This game will test your powers of recall. There are several ways to play it. One method is to collect a number of objects (ten to fifteen). These are put on a flat surface or in a box and the players are given one minute in which to study them. The box is then put out of sight and the players have one minute to write down the name of every object they can remember. The winner is the player with the longest list.

Another way to play this is for a non-player to draw ten different shapes on a piece of paper. These should not be too complicated. After a few moments study the players have to draw as many shapes as accurately as they can. The winner is the player with the most shapes, correctly drawn.

A third method is to write down the names of objects such as a cotton reel, a paper bag, a currant bun. The paper is then hidden and the players write down the names of the objects. Sometimes it is the simplest items that catch people out. It is easier to remember a bright pink dragon-shaped brooch than a paper clip!

SIMON SAYS

Younger players really enjoy this. Although it is better suited to a railway carriage or boat it can be played in smaller spaces by making the actions more restricted. A leader begins by saying 'Simon says do this'. He or she makes a movement which is copied by the other players. This could be shutting one eye or patting the top of the head. The action continues until the leader changes the order. Every instruction must begin with 'Simon says'. If if does not the players do not change the movement but carry on with the previous instruction. The idea is to keep the game going at a good speed so that the players are caught out more easily. The game goes on until just one player is left. They then become the leader.

GROUP STORIES

This is an entertaining way of passing the time on a boring journey. Every member of a group contributes to a story which can be as clever or as silly as you want to make it. There are several ways in which a group story can be created. A good way to start is the One Word Story. You should not allow too much time for this story, two minutes at the most, as it needs to rattle along at quite a fast pace.

Each member of the group adds one word at a time to the tale. No one should stop to think for too long as it spoils the rhythm. Stop whenever you feel that the story has got too boring.

This game can also be extended to sentences. Everyone adds a sentence to the story, but if someone hesitates too long they are out and the next player takes over. You many now be ready to progress to a more difficult group story.

The Cliff Hanger

This game gives all the players lots of scope for their imagination. This time each player can contribute as much as they like to a story, within reason, but they must end their section on a note of suspense. The idea is to make it as difficult as possible for the next person to follow. The story could sound like this:

First player: 'One night, as I was lying in my bed I heard . . .'
Second player: '. . . the ringing of a bell. It sounded as if it was coming from the attic. I put on my slippers and crept along the landing. Suddenly I saw a large . . .'
Third player: '. . . spider! It ran away as I pulled down the attic ladder. Slowly I climbed up and just as my head drew level with the open attic door I caught sight of . . .'
First player: '. . . my face in an old mirror.'

And so on. If you can, it is great fun to record these stories.

SIXTY SECOND SOAP BOX

There are occasions when sixty seconds may seem like a very long time. Each player is given a theme. All you have to do is speak for one minute on that subject, without hesitating, repeating yourself or going off the subject. Other players may challenge you at any time if they feel that you are guilty of one of these things.

A good way to start is to allow players to choose their own topics for the first round. If everyone manages one minute a non-player should choose the winner, who should be the player who has spoken the most eloquently on their chosen subject.

After this a selection of subjects can be written on a list numbered from one to ten. Each player calls a number and the subject at that number will become their theme. Here are some ideas for topics.

My pet hate.
What I would do if I were Prime Minister.
The best dinner that I have ever had.
How I would spend £1,000.
My room.

LAST LETTER

The longer you play this game the more difficult it becomes. First of all you choose a fairly general sort of category. This could be boys' or girls' names, countries, animals or song titles. The first player says a name within the chosen category. If this were girls' names he or she may say Laura. The next player must also say a name but it must begin with the last letter of the name just mentioned, Ann for example.

As you become more skilful you will find ways to catch the other players out. Many girls' names, for example, end with the letter 'y', but not many begin with it. If you keep saying names which end in 'y' your partner may give in more quickly. The game goes on until someone is unable to think of another name. The last person able to say a name will be the winner. You could also play this game as a group and see how long you can keep it going.

FORTUNATELY/UNFORTUNATELY

This is a story-telling game in which all the players contribute in turn.

One player begins a story by saying:

'Fortunately I have won first prize in a raffle.'

The next player must begin:

'But unfortunately the prize was a hippopotamus.'

The next player continues:

'But fortunately my uncle owns a zoo.'

It is quite likely that the next player will say that the zoo has closed down. If anyone hesitates or repeats something they are out. Each addition must be in keeping with the story. The important thing is that each contribution turns the story around. The story will get more and more complicated as each player tries to extricate himself from a difficult situation. The game can go on as long as you like or until someone is unable to continue – unfortunately!

YES AND NO

Do you realize how hard it is to avoid saying yes or no? This game will show you how difficult it really is. The object of the game is to last for one minute without saying yes or no. To make this more difficult the other players will be firing questions at you constantly. Each question must be answered. Nodding or shaking of the head also counts as yes or no, so does answering in a foreign language! You will also be out if you hesitate for too long.

If more than one player lasts the minute there can be another round.

ALPHABET SOUP

This alphabet game requires quick thinking as the winner is the first person to call out a correct answer. A non-player holds the list below. Each player calls out in turn a number and then a letter.

The non-player reads out the category indicated by the number. The players have to think of a word in this category that begins with the chosen letter. The first person to call out an acceptable answer wins a point. The game goes on until one player has five points. If the first player calls '4 H' somebody may call out helicopter, for example; 9 P could be potato, 17 W could be a washing machine. Be careful though, saying 'daddy' for 18 D may not go down well.

1 Something white
2 A song
3 An item of sports equipment
4 Something that flies
5 Something that lives in water
6 Something found on a beach
7 Something that makes music
8 An item of furniture
9 Something that grows
10 Something that smells
11 An indoor game
12 A sportsman
13 Something round
14 Something square
15 Something that can be worn
16 Something that has fur
17 Something automatic
18 Something more than 100 years old
19 Something cold
20 An entertainer

You can add some categories of your own. Each player must say a different number each time so you may need to cross the numbers off on a piece of paper so that a record is kept of the numbers that have already been used. Any arguments should be settled by the non-player holding the list.

AROUND THE WORLD

This is a game for real alphabet experts. The first player asks the second player, 'Where are you going?' The answer must be a country. The questioner then asks , 'What will you do there?'

Now comes the tricky part. Every word in the answer must begin with the same letter as the country – and still make sense.

Supposing the answer to the first question was 'China', the answer to the second question might be, 'Chew cucumbers crossly.'

If the first answer was 'Portugal' the second might be, 'Paint parrots' and so on. The second answer should be as imaginative as possible but still make some sort of sense. After a couple of rounds a non-player could decide which answer was the most inventive. The answers may be at random or, if you wish to make it harder, in strict alphabetical order.

GOING TO MARKET

Money is no object in this game. Each player begins their turn by saying, 'I went to market and I bought . . .'. The player then mentions any item as long as it is in alphabetical order. The first player might say, 'I went to market and I bought some artichokes.' The second player might continue by saying, 'I went to market and I bought some balloons.' The third player might continue with, 'I went to market and I bought some carrots', and so on.

The game gets harder when you come to letters such as 'y' and 'z'.

With younger players it is best to keep to one item at a time. The game becomes more demanding if each player has to remember all the items which have gone before as well as make up a new one of their own. If they forget any of the items then they are out of the game.

SILENT SPELLING

This is a memory, spelling and action game all rolled into one. Each player is given a word to spell. This is not done in the usual way but in a mixture of actions and letters. The player is allowed to say any of the consonants in his or her word out loud. All the vowels are mimed. You can make up your own mimes or use the following suggestions.

A Raise the right arm.
E Clap your hands.
I Point to yourself.
O Form a circle with your arms.
U Point to another player.

If the word is 'Hear', for example, the player will say H then clap, raise his right arm and finish by saying R.

If you wish to make the game more challenging you could add some further rules. B could be a buzzing sound, M a mooing sound, W a wave of the hand and so on. As it is quite hard work remembering all the actions it is best to keep the spellings quite simple until everyone is used to the game.

If all the actions are correct and the spelling is right the player scores a point. This could also, in a bigger space, be played in teams.

THE HOUSE THAT JACK BUILT

This game builds on a single statement just as the nursery rhyme does. It can be played in pairs or in a group. The first player makes a statement. This could be, 'I have a cat.' The next player extends this idea so he or she might say, 'I have a dog who chases the cat.' This could be followed by, 'I have a cousin who owns the dog who chases the cat.'

The game can become as silly as you like. The

fourth player might add, 'I have a picture of a gorilla painted by the cousin, etc.

Every player must remember what has gone before and repeat it in the correct order. This can become very tricky after a while and also very funny if players get themselves mixed up.

SPECIAL EFFECTS
Two or more players

If you have a good storyteller amongst your fellow travellers this game can be great fun. First of all you need to choose five things which make some kind of noise. These might be duck (quack, quack), an alarm clock (ding-a-ling), a car (brmm, brmm), a donkey (hee-haw) and a leaky tap (drip, drip). These sounds are then distributed among the players. The storyteller must tell a story in which these items occur quite regularly. As soon as any of the players hears their object or animal mentioned they must make the appropriate sound. This can be played just for fun or as a competitive game. If you wish to play it as the latter the storyteller must try to catch the players out so that they miss coming in at the right moment. If they miss their sound they are out and another player has to take it on. It can end up with one player having to remember all five sounds.

TABOO
Two or more players

There are two ways to play this game, one a little harder than the other. The simpler way is to choose a word that comes up quite often when we speak. This word then becomes 'Taboo'. If any of the players say the word they are out. The word could be 'the' or 'you' or 'and'. One player then questions the others and tries to make them say the forbidden word.

The second method makes a letter 'Taboo' and every word which contains it has to be avoided. The players are questioned by the leader and anyone who hesitates too long is out. When a player is out they become the question-master until they manage to get another player to say the 'Taboo' letter.

THE PROPS GAME

Collect together a few small items – five is a good number – and put them in a bag or a box. All sorts of bits and pieces could be included: string, a wrapped sweet, a purse, a safety pin, etc. Whatever the objects, the idea of the game is to incorporate them into a story. The story can be any length. The only rule is that each item must be introduced separately. You cannot get around the problem by saying 'And when I opened the box I found a piece of string, a sweet . . . etc'.

When everyone has had a turn a non-player can decide which has been the most inventive.

An alternative way to play the game is to give each player an object. They each have to include this object in their part of a group story. If suitable items are not readily available you could write the names of some everyday objects on pieces of paper and distribute them.

PENCIL TO PAPER

SPROUTS
Two players

Three or four dots are drawn onto a piece of paper. Each player takes it in turns to draw a line which connects any two dots or one dot to itself. The line does not have to be straight. It can loop or curve or squiggle! Once you have drawn the line a new dot is placed on it. This sounds easy but there are a few rules which make it more difficult. Firstly, no line must cross another or be drawn across itself. Secondly, no dot must have more than three lines coming out from it. It will make it easier if you draw a line through a dot once it has sprouted three lines. The player who makes the last possible move is the winner.

1st move   *2nd move*   *3rd move*

INVENT A CLUE
Two players

Squared paper is very useful for this game but, failing this you will need to draw out a nine by nine grid. The object is to create your own crossword without any clues. The first player writes a word anywhere on the grid. A point is scored for every letter. It may be easier to have a pencil of a different colour for the second player, who then writes in a word of his own. This must connect with the first player's word. Points may only be scored for new letters. Using letters which are already on the grid does not count. When neither player can continue the points are added up. The winner is the player with the most points.

Now that you have created a crossword, why don't you make up some clues and number your grid, and see if someone else can manage to do it.

T	O		O		S			A
R			C		T	O	W	N
A	T		T	E	A			G
V			O		M			E
E			P	E	P	P	E	R
L			U		I			
S	A	U	S	A	G	E	S	
	I			D		R	E	D
	R	E	A	D	Y		A	

PICTURE CONSEQUENCES
Two to four players

There are no winners in this game. It is played strictly for fun.

Fold a piece of paper into four sections. The first player, out of sight of the others, draws a head and the start of a neck. The paper is folded so that only a small section of neck may be seen. The next player draws the top half of the body and the arms. The third player draws from the waist to the knees and finally the last artist draws the legs and feet. The body may be split into thirds or fifths depending on the number of players but you need to decide where one section stops and the other begins.

Try and make your section as inventive as you can. The results when the paper is unfolded can be hilarious. You may discover an elephant wearing a kilt and wellington boots!

THE LIST GAME
Two or more players

This is an excellent game for travelling. Any number of people can play – and adults enjoy it as much as children. Each player has a piece of paper on which they write a list of categories: boy's names, girl's names, animals, towns, fruits, colours, etc. . Everyone can help to decide these. When you have chosen about ten categories, a letter is chosen by randomly pointing at a book or newspaper. It is not really a good idea to have a letter such as 'z', however, and you might like to change this!

At a given signal everybody frantically starts to fill in words which begin with the chosen letter for each item on the list. This could be played against the clock (say, two minutes) or until everyone has given up. Everybody announces their word for each item on the list. If you have thought of a word that no one else has thought of, you get two points. Otherwise each word will score one point.

It is amazing how your mind goes blank when you first start to play this game. As you become more expert you could try making the categories harder. For instance you could include, characters in books by Lewis Carroll, insects, furry animals, etc.

HANGMAN
Two players

This is the sort of game which really makes you wonder who thought it up! Perhaps some bored prisoner as he sat in his cell. Anyway, the race to beat the Hangman can be very exciting. One player thinks of a word (that he knows how to spell). He draws the same number of dashes on a piece of paper as there are letters.

At the foot of the paper the alphabet is written out. This is not necessary but can be helpful, especially for younger players. The second player then calls out various letters. If they are part of the word they are written in their correct place. Every time an incorrect letter is called out a part of the gallows is drawn. The idea is to guess the word before the gallows are complete and you are 'hanged'. There are variations on the shape of the gallows but most look something like this. The numbers show the order in which it is drawn.

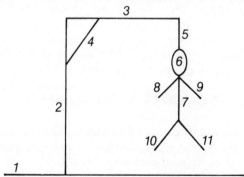

As each letter is called it is helpful to cross them off the alphabet at the bottom of the page. If the word is very difficult you could give the guesser more of a chance by adding on hands and feet, or even a face, to the picture.

HANGMAN VARIATIONS

Hangman By Theme
This is played in the same way as Hangman but with titles or names instead of single words. You could decide beforehand on a theme such as Films.

To make it more difficult two parts of the gallows are drawn for every incorrect guess.

Hangman Doubles
In this variation both players choose a word and take it in turn to guess each other's. It is not always a good idea to choose long words as these are easier to guess. Sometimes short words such as 'ski' can really puzzle an opponent.

DOT TO DOT
Two players
This game is a real test for your imagination. Each player draws between ten and twenty dots onto a piece of paper. The players then swop papers. The challenge is to draw a picture by joining the dots. If it proves to be very difficult an agreed number of extra dots may be added. The winner is the player who produces the most imaginative drawing.

NOUGHTS AND CROSSES
Two players
The traditional game of noughts and crosses is played on a grid made from two pairs of parallel lines, one horizontal and one vertical.

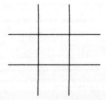

One player will draw noughts and the other crosses. The object is to place three noughts or three crosses in a row. Each player tries to stop the other from doing this by blocking any lines which may be winners. The winning line may be drawn in any direction, horizontally, vertically or diagonally.

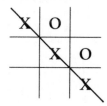

If this becomes too easy you can make the game more interesting by closing in the sides and using the corners and putting the noughts and crosses where the lines cross. Three in a row still wins.

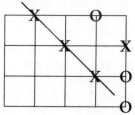

FIVE IN A ROW
Two to four players

This game can be played on all sorts of surfaces – peg boards, graph paper – anything that is marked into squares. Each player chooses a shape, counter or colour. The players take it in turns to put their mark on the paper or board. The object is to get five in any row, in any direction.

This may sound simple but the game can go on for a very long time.

					O	X	
				X	O	△	
		O	O	X	O	△	
			O	O	O	△	
			X	X	X	△	O
						△	

BOXES

This can be played on squared or plain paper. Mark out a square or rectangle like the one below, using dots. It can be any size you like – but the larger the pattern the longer the game will be. The players take it in turns to join the dots. The object is to try and join up the fourth line of any square. The square or box then becomes yours and your initial is put inside it. When all the dots have been joined the player with the most initialled boxes is the winner.

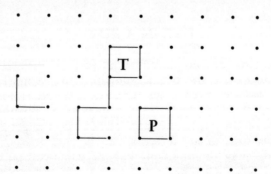

WORMS
Two players

For this game you need to mark out a square or rectangles of dots as you would do for boxes. The first player joins any two dots together with a straight line, horizontally or vertically but not diagonally. The second player continues a line from one of these dots to another. The idea is to force the other player into a situation where the line or 'worm' joins back onto itself.

BATTLESHIPS
Two players

Each player needs two pieces of squared paper marked with a 10 by 10 grid. One of these will be used for the home fleet and one for the enemy fleet. Each fleet is made up of six submarines, four destroyers, two cruisers, and one battleship. Each player places these horizontally or vertically but they must not touch each other. The letters A–J are written across the top of each grid. The numbers 1–10 are written down the left hand side. You must not see the other player's pieces of paper.

Now the battle commences! The first player chooses a square and calls out the grid number (e.g. C5). The second player looks at his grid to see if he has a ship on that square. If it is empty he says 'Nothing'. If it is a hit he must say the name of the ship (e.g. destroyer).

The players take it in turns to fire shots. The spare grid is used to help you find the enemy fleet. You should know that all the squares immediately surrounding a ship will be empty. Mark the enemy ships with a cross and it will be easier to find the others. The battle continues until one whole fleet has been sunk. You can adapt this game if you wish to include all sorts of ships.

	A	B	C	D	E	F	G	H	I	J
1					C	C	C			
2										S
3	C		D	D						
4	C					D		D	D	
5	C					D				
6										
7			S							
8	S						D	D		S
9					S					
10			S				B	B	B	B

Each submarine occupies one square, each destroyer two squares, each cruiser three squares and each battleship four squares.

UNSEEN ART
Two or more players

This game is a test of your ability to draw without looking. You can either play it with paper resting on a book on top of your head (which looks incredibly silly but is fun to do) or with your eyes shut tightly. First you must choose your subject. It should be something simple, with clear outlines. It could be a cat, a house or a pig. Draw it onto a piece of paper so that the players know what they should be aiming to produce. Now comes the tricky bit! With eyes shut or with the paper on your head you must try and draw the picture as well as you can.

When everyone has finished you can either choose the best one by agreement – or it might be safer to get a non-player to decide.

WORDS, WORDS, WORDS

JUMBLIES

You will need a pencil and paper for this game. Each player thinks of a title from a film, a book or a song. First of all the title is written down with all the letters running together like this:

Thewindinthewillows.

The players then break their letters to make a strange looking sentence:

T hew indin t hewi llows.

At a given signal all the players swop over their papers. The winner is the first player to write out the title in the correct way:

The Wind in the Willows.

It is amazing how odd some really well known titles look when they are written like this. See if you can unjumble some of the following:

Y ouon lyl iv et wice

Fu ngu sth eb og eym an

On ema nwen t tom ow

A lic ei nwond erl and

Hi cko ryd icko ryd o ck

GHOST

Two to four players

The object of this game is avoid becoming Ghost!

It is not as supernatural as it sounds. This is a word building game in which players must try to avoid being the one to complete a word. The first player chooses the first letter of a word. This might be 'e' (thinking of 'enjoy'). The second player may think of 'excite' and say 'x'. The next player could say 'a' with 'examine' in mind. As a possible word emerges the trick is to try and direct the shape of the word so that you do not have to finish it. If, for example, you realize that the word 'examine' would finish on your turn, you should try to turn it into 'examination' by putting an 'a' where the 'e' should have been. You must not say just any letter that comes into your head. You should always have a word in mind which you could say if another player challenges you. If you do not have a dictionary with you a non-player should referee if there is a disagreement.

TIN TEN TON
Two or more players

You will need pencil and paper for this game. You choose a combination of the following letters 'tin', 'ten' or 'ton'. The idea of the game is to collect as many words as possible which contain those letters, in the correct order. If you chose 'tin' for example your list might include sting, continent, hitting, exciting, tinsel.

You could either carry on until everyone has given up or set a time limit of five minutes.

There are plenty of other three letter combinations which you might like to choose from such as cat, son, hit, lot, fun, din and win.

CLAP, CLAP, CLAP, CLICK

This is a word association game which can be played by two people or in a larger group. After three slow claps everybody clicks their fingers. As they do this the first player says a word, on the click. This rhythm is kept up throughout the game and each player in turn has to say a word as everyone clicks their fingers. The word must have some association with the word which has gone before. At any time a player can be challenged for their choice of word. If they cannot justify it they are out. The word must be said on the click or the player can be challenged for hesitation. The game could go like this:

'Clap, clap, clap, fish.'
'Clap, clap, clap, fingers.'
'Clap, clap, clap, ring.'
'Clap, clap, clap, circus.'

WORD WIMBLEDON
Two players

Here is a way to play tennis without moving. Instead of hitting a ball backwards and forwards you use words instead. The scoring is just the same as tennis. The first player begins by saying a word. The next follows on with another which must have some association with the first. The first player to hesitate, repeat himself or say a word not associated with the one which has gone before loses the point. The score will then stand at fifteen-love. Once the game has been won play can then carry on into sets. You can play a three set or a five set match, depending on how much time you have.

BARGAIN BOOKS

Have you every thought of writing a book? In this game you can make a start by writing the title page. The idea is to create a title and an author and to make the match as funny as possible. Here are a few examples:

Let's Go Out by R.U. Ready
The Science Of Explosives by Di Nomite
How To Make Money by I.M. Rich
Thirty Minute Stories by R. Fanhour
Never Take Chances by Justin Case
Road Transport by Laurie Driver
Try And Try Again by Percy Vere
The Calypso Band by Lydia Dustbin

PICTURE A WORD

This game is played just for fun. The idea is to draw a word in such a way that the picture shows the meaning. If you like a bit of competition someone who is not taking part could select the most imaginative effort. You certainly do not need to be a great artist – it is the idea that counts. Below are some examples of the sort of designs which reflect a meaning.

ALL SQUARE

Two players

Each player draws a grid composed of six vertical and six horizontal lines, to create twenty-five boxes. The first player then calls out a letter. Both players write this letter on their grid in any box they choose. The next player calls out another letter. Play continues with the players calling out alternate letters until all twenty-five boxes are filled.

The idea of the game is to make as many words as possible on the grid. The same letter may be called out several times as each player tries to steer the game in their favour. At the end of the game each player adds up the score by counting the number of words they have made horizontally or vertically. A five letter word scores the maximum – ten points, a four letter word five points and a three letter word one point.

BANGERS AND MASH

When you are bored with reading a book, magazine or newspaper this game provides a way to liven things up. An extract is chosen from a book or newspaper and somebody reads it out loud. The reader has to remember the only rule of this game. Every time he or she comes to a word beginning with 'b' it must be changed to 'bangers' and every word beginning with 'm' to 'mash'. You can make the menu a bit wider if you wish. For all the words beginning with 'c' you say 'chips' and all the 'g's become 'gravy'. You really have to concentrate hard. If the listeners hear you say a word beginning with these letters without the correct substitution they must call out and take over the story themselves.

DEFINITELY NOT

Two or more players

This game may be played anywhere, as long as you have a dictionary with you. It will not only stretch your acting ability but also teach you the meanings of some extraordinary words. Each player chooses a word from the dictionary and writes it down. It is then shown to the other players. The idea is to choose a word which the other players will never have heard of. Each player then gives a definition of their word. It can be as long or involved as the player wishes to make it. The other players then have to decide whether the definition is a true one or whether the player has made it up. All the players who guess correctly score a point. Any player who manages to fool all the other players scores a bonus point. Here are some words that might fox the opposition: feoffee, limitrophe, mangonel, misoneism, skippet, xoanon, zemindar.

This is also a good game to play in a large group which can be divided into teams. Each member of the team gives a different definition of the same word and the opposing side has to guess which one is correct.

BRIDGE THE WORD
Two or more players
Each player draws six lines across a piece of paper. Somebody then chooses a six-letter word and this is written vertically with each letter at the beginning of a line. The word is also written at the end of each line but this time it begins at the bottom line. If the chosen word was 'listed' the result would like like this:

L	D
I	E
S	T
T E L E C O M M U N I C A T I O N S	
E	I
D	L

The game is a race to see who can bridge the word most successfully. Each player tries to think of a word which starts with the letter at the start of the line and ends with the letter at the end. The player with the longest word for each of the six combinations wins a point. It is best to set a time limit of five minutes for this game.

THERE AND BACK

Can you change a nose into eyes? Or beer into wine? Here is your chance to perform some word magic. You begin with one word and in a series of steps transform it into another. At each step you may change one letter of the word but it must always remain a real word. The idea is to make the change in as few moves as possible. Once you have transformed your word you can then challenge your opponents to try and do it in fewer steps. Here is how 'wolf' is transformed into 'lamb':

Wolf
Golf
Gold
Sold
Sole
Sale
Sane
Lane
Lame
Lamb

You could use three-letter words to begin with. Make up your own combinations and see who can transform them the fastest. Here are a few more suggestions: Cow into Pig; Frog into Toad; Ill into Fit; Kiss into Slap; Mud into Gem.

EXPANDING WORDS
Two or more players

The object of the game is to create as long a word as you can, starting with a one-letter word. You are only allowed to add one letter at a time and at each step a real word must be made. Although you cannot change the order of the letters the new letter can be added anywhere.

Everybody starts with 'A' or 'I'. When the players

have created the longest word they can then tell their opponents their final word. Then everybody has to try to work back to the original letter. Here are two examples of word building:

A	A
At	Am
Fat	Ham
Flat	Sham
Float	Shame
Afloat	Shamed
	Ashamed

CONSEQUENCES

There are several ways to play this game. As in Picture consequences each player contributes to the whole without knowing what the other players have done. The most common way of playing it is to divide a piece of paper into eight or nine sections. These represent sections of a story and follow a sequence which is decided beforehand. The sequence might be:

1 A name with a short description of the person.
2 Another name with a description.
3 The place where they met.
4 How they met.
5 What the first person said to the second person.
6 The second person's reply.
7 What happened next.
8 What everybody said about it.
9 The consequences.

You could add or take away sections if you wished. Depending on the number of players, it may be necessary for some sections to be written by the same person. This does not matter as long as they are not following on from one to the other. Try to make each section as inventive as possible as this adds to the fun when the paper is unravelled and the whole story read out.

Variation On Consequences

If you do not have much time there is a shorter version which can be very amusing. Divide a piece of paper into five columns. Across the top of the page write these headings:

Adjective   Noun   Verb   Adjective   Noun

The first player then writes down five adjectives in the first column and folds the paper lengthwise so that they cannot be seen. The second player fills in five nouns and also folds back the paper.

When all the columns have been filled the paper is opened out and someone reads across the page, turning the words into a sentence by adding joining words such as 'and'; 'the' or 'in'. If, for example, the first line reads happy onion jumped murky television, it might become, The happy onion jumped over the murky television.

BACK TO FRONT
Two or more players

Although it is quite easy to count backwards, it is much harder to do the same thing with letters. All the players have to try to say the alphabet beginning with 'z' and working back to 'a'. A non-player could judge which attempt was the best or you could time each effort and see who can do it the fastest.

You will then be ready to progress to the next stage. Each player is given a nursery rhyme to say. Backwards of course! The first line of the rhyme becomes the last and so on.

The really ambitious could try to sing a song backwards. This is very difficult as you have to remember the tune as well as the words. Have a try and see how far you can get. This can be great fun if played in a group with each member supplying a different line.

ANAGRAMS
Two or more players

The strange thing about anagrams is that complicated words are often easier to unscramble than simple ones. In this game all the players are given the same set of anagrams to solve. The first player to work them all out is the winner. You could put a time limit on the game if you wish and see who has the most correct answers at the end.

The anagrams should have a theme of some sort, colours or fruits for example, so that the players have some idea of what to look for.

This can also be played as a team game. Each team makes up a set of anagrams and challenges the other team to work them out. An amusing theme would be the names of mutual friends. You could challenge each other to make up the funniest anagram using their names.

GROUP POEMS
Two or more players

Four words are chosen at the beginning of this game. The first must rhyme with the third and the second with the fourth. These will become the last words in each line of a poem. One player begins and makes up the first line. Another player writes the second and the paper is passed around until the poem is complete. You can decide whether each player is allowed to see the line which has gone before or not. Supposing the four chosen words were star, sky, car and pie, the poem may come out like this:

'I dreamt I saw a falling star.'
'Way up in the sky.'
'But when I stepped out of my car.'
'It became a custard pie.'

Well, perhaps poem is rather a kind word for it –
but at least it rhymes!

WORD SQUARES

Are you a whizz with words? This game will test
your ingenuity. You play it by yourself and you can
leave it and come back to it whenever you want to.
The idea is to make a square from words which read
the same both across and downwards. First of all
you must decide how big you would like the square
to be. Four by four is the best size to start with:

B	A	T	S
A	R	E	A
T	E	A	M
S	A	M	E

MATCH THE WORD
Two or more players

This is a very simple game which can be played
individually or in teams. A non-player says a word
or a name which is usually associated with another
word or name. The first player to call out the word
it should be matched with wins the point. For
example: fish and chips; black and white; egg and
bacon; king and queen; Jekyll and Hyde; Cain and
Abel.

Where a word could possibly be matched by two other words the person starting each pair must decide whether to accept the alternative. This happens, for example, with 'bread' which goes with 'butter' and 'jam'.

TONGUE TWISTERS

Tangling your tongue around some tortuous twisters is a good way to pass the time on a journey. About two hundred years ago these tricky little rhymes were sometimes used in schools to help children learn how to speak correctly. Today you can have lots of fun repeating them faster and faster whilst trying to keep the words clear. You could even make some up and challenge your friends to repeat them. Try these:

Red leather, yellow leather.

She sells sea shells by the sea shore.
The shells that she sells are sea shells, I'm sure.

Six thick thistle sticks.

Swan swam over the sea
Swim swan swim
Swan swam back again
Well swum swan.

A proper cup of coffee from a proper coffee pot.

What noise annoys a noisy oyster?
A noisy noise annoys a noisy oyster.

Run the washing, Russell.

Some shun sunshine.
Do you shun sunshine?

A big black bug bit a big black bear
And the big black bear bled blood.

Peter Piper picked a peck of pickled peppers.
A peck of pickled peppers Peter Piper picked
If Peter Piper picked a peck of pickled peppers
Where's the peck of pickled peppers Peter Piper
  picked?

Cross crossings cautiously

Esau Wood sawed wood,
Esau Wood sawed wood,
All the wood that Esau saw
With a wood saw would saw wood.

CRACK THE CODE

Journeys give you lots of opportunity to let your imagination take over. Pretend you are not really going to see Granny but you are a spy escaping in the back seat of a stolen car. Or you are a pirate sailing across the sea with a sword tucked under your anorak. It's great fun pretending and this game can become part of one of your adventures.

Anyone travelling in secret may have to make contact with someone else. How do you let that person know who are are without anyone else finding out? You must make up a message in code.

Start off with some very simple codes:

evI tog a teckcap fo steews.

Each word is simply reversed – I've got a packet of sweets. Or you could reverse the whole sentence:

steews fo teckcap a tog evI.

In this code 'A' = 'Z', 'B' = 'Y' and so on.

REV TLG Z KZXPVG LU HDVVGH

Or you could move every letter along once so that 'A' becomes 'B' and so on.

JWF FPU B QBDLFU PG TXFFUT

You could even write the message in numbers with A = 1, B = 2, etc.

DICE & CARDS

BEGGAR MY NEIGHBOUR
Two to six players

In this game the object is to win all the cards. When all the cards have been dealt the players must not look at them. Each player takes it in turn to place a card, face up, on a central pile. Play continues in this way until a picture card is turned up. The player to the left of the person who laid the picture card then has to 'pay' a certain number of cards to him or her. If the card was an Ace four cards must be handed over, a King is worth three cards a Queen two cards and a Jack, one card. It is possible, however, to reverse the situation if the 'payment' includes a picture card. If this occurs the next player on the left has to pay back the correct number of cards to his neighbour. Depending on the way the cards fall, this game can go on for a long time. It may be a good idea to put a time limit on the game and see who has the most cards at the end of the time.

PATIENCE

There are times, when everyone has fallen asleep or is looking out of a window, when it is good to have a game to play by yourself. Patience is an ideal game for one player. There are many different forms but, it you have never played before, here is a simple version. First of all, take out of the pack any cards higher than a seven plus the Aces. Shuffle the cards and deal them out, face up, in front of you. As you put down each card say seven, eight, nine, ten, Jack, Queen, King, Ace. If the card that you put down and the name you say are the same, put the card to one side. The idea is to get rid of all your cards in this way. After going through the pack once, shuffle the cards and continue where you left off. You only lose if you go through the pack without losing any of your cards.

THIRTY ONE
Ten to four players
This game will improve your maths as you have to add up very quickly. The object is to have three cards of one suit which will add up to thirty-one. The next best hand is three cards of the same value. Three Aces have the highest value and three twos the least. Aces count as eleven, picture cards as ten and all the other cards according to their value.

Each player is dealt three cards. Three cards are also dealt, face up, in the middle of the players. The first player exchanges one of his or her cards for one from the middle. When one of the players thinks that his or her hand will beat all the others he or she says, 'Call'. The players are then allowed one more turn before showing their cards. You can play any number of rounds that you choose, adding the score as you go along.

CRAZY EIGHTS
Two to four players
This is an exciting game. A player may just be about to win and find victory snatched away at the last minute. Eight cards are dealt to each player. One card is turned over from the remaining pile. The player to the left of the dealer must place a card of the same suit, face up, on top of this card. If this is not possible, he or she must take a card from the central pile. It is possible to change the suit, however, by placing a card of a different suit but the same value on top of the last card to be played.

Certain cards change the rules. If you play a Jack

you can also play another card of the same suit. If you have two Jacks, you may play three cards altogether. If a player puts down a two the next player must pick up two cards. The only way to avoid this is by putting down another two. The next player then has to pick up four cards, etc. The Queen of Spades also means that the following player must pick up four cards. Eights are always wild. Any player who puts down an eight can decide what the suit will be. The winner is the first player to get rid of all his or her cards.

CHEAT
Two to four players

At last – a game in which you can cheat as much as you like. In fact the more the better!

The object of the game is to be the first one to get rid of all your cards. All the cards are dealt between the players until one card is left. This card is placed, face up, in the middle. It is quite helpful to sort out your hands into suits before you begin. The idea is that each card must follow suit. As the cards are laid face down players can lay down any card they like without being caught out – unless an opponent happens to call out 'Cheat!' In this case you must show your card. If it is the correct suit the caller has to pick up all the cards. If you have cheated, however, you have to pick up all the cards. The player who has picked up the cards starts a new suit.

ENFLAY
Two players

Before play begins all the twos, threes, fours, fives and sixes are removed from the pack. Thirty-two cards should be left. Each player has eight cards and the remainder are placed face down. The first player puts a card from his hand face up on a flat surface.

The other player must play a card of the same suit. These cards are then put to one side. The player who laid the higher of the two cards plays the next card, which must be of a different suit. If this cannot be matched by the second player a card is taken from the central pile. The winner is the first player to get rid of all his or her cards.

PERSIAN CARDS
Two players

This is a very simple game. It is particularly good for beginners at card games, as it helps them to recognize suits. The pack is divided equally between two players. Aces are high. At the same moment both players turn over a card. If the cards are of the same suit the higher card beats the lower in value. The player who laid the higher card then takes all the cards which have been turned up. The player who succeeds in taking all the cards is the winner.

GO FISH
Two players

Each player begins this game with seven cards. The rest of the pack is placed, face down, in front of them. The object is to form sets of cards made up of four cards of the same value, e.g. four sixes. If the first player has an eight in his hand he may say to his opponent 'Give me your eights'. If the other player has some eights in his hand he must hand them over. If he does not he says, 'Go fish'. The first player then has to pick up a card from the pile. When a player has managed to collect four cards of the same value he puts them down in front of him. The winner is the player with the most sets at the end of the game.

To make things easier for younger players it is possible to play this game in pairs.

CRAG
Two or more players
Three dice

This is a game which appears to be more complicated than it really is. It does need a little preparation as you have to make a score sheet.

	Player 1	Player 2	Player 3
Ones			
Twos			
Threes			
Fours			
Fives			
Sixes			
Odd straight			
Even straight			
Low straight			
High straight			
Three of a kind			
Thirteen			
·Crag			
Totals			

This can be adapted to any number of players but is more fun with two or three. Each player throws to see who will start. The one with the highest score begins. He has to try to score one of the patterns on the score sheet. If the players wish one or two dice may be thrown instead of three. The points are scored as follows.

Ones One point for each one thrown. Three points.
Twos Two points for each two thrown. Maximum six points.
Threes Three points for each three shown. Maximum nine points.
Fours Four points for each four thrown. Maximum twelve points.
Fives Five points for each five thrown. Maximum fifteen points.
Sixes Six points for each six thrown. Maximum eighteen points.
Odd straight 1, 3, 5. Twenty points.
Even straight 2, 4, 6. Twenty points.
Low straight 1, 2, 3. Twenty points.
High straight 4, 5, 6. Twenty points.
Three of a kind All the dice showing the same value. Twenty-five points.
Thirteen Any combination which adds up to 13 as long as there are no doubles. 3, 4 and 6 for example. Twenty-six points.
Crag Any combination which adds up to thirteen including a double – 1, 6, 6 for example. Fifty points.

Each player throws the dice in turn and enters his score on the scoresheet. Sometimes there may be a choice of score. If, for instance, a player throws two sixes and a four he will probably choose the twelve points for the double six rather than the four points for the four. However, if he has already scored a pattern of sixes he will have to choose the four. The dice are passed round thirteen times. If a player is unable to score one of the patterns he must decide on his turn which section to leave blank. The winner is the player with the greatest number of points at the end.

FIFTY
Two dice
Two or more players

In this game you are only allowed to score if you throw a double. You do this by throwing two dice showing the same value. If a double six is thrown twenty points are scored. Every other double, except three, counts as five points. A double three is very bad news as the player loses all his previous score. This can be very annoying when you are on the verge of winning. Play continues until one player has managed to score fifty points.

SEQUENCES
Two or more players
Three dice

Each player draws a scoresheet which looks like this:

1	2	3	4	5	6	7	8	9	10	11	12
12	11	10	9	8	7	6	5	4	3	2	1

The idea of the game is to cross off the numbers on the scoresheet in the correct order. When you have crossed off the numbers 1–12 you repeat the sequence in the reverse order, from 12–1.

The first player throws three dice. A one must be

thrown before any player is allowed to start. The player does not only cross off the numbers shown on the dice but can also add up the numbers. For example, if 1, 2 and 3 are thrown, these may be crossed off the scoresheet. Then as $1 + 3 = 4$, $2 + 3 = 5$, and $1 + 2 + 3 = 6$, 4, 5 and 6 may be crossed off as well. Remember that the numbers must be crossed off in order. If you are unable to do this the dice are passed to the next player.

There are variations on this game. In the game of 'Everest' the numbers do not have to be thrown in sequence and so it is much faster.

GOING TO BOSTON
Two or more players
Three dice + pencil and paper

The object of this game is to be the first player to score 100. The first player throws three dice and puts the one with the highest score to one side. Then the player throws two dice and sets aside the higher of the two. After a final throw all the scores are totalled. Players can win a bonus of thirty points if the first throw is three of a kind. Two of a kind on the second throw earns a player an extra fifteen points. Each player throws in turn until someone manages to 'get to Boston' by scoring 100.

HAIL TO YOUR MAJESTY
Two to six players

This game requires a good memory as well as a fast hand. The cards are shuffled and dealt between the players. Each player puts his cards face down. The players take it in turns to place a card face up on a central pile. If a King is turned up the first player to say, 'Hail to your Majesty' wins the cards. When a Queen is turned up the greeting is, 'Good Morning, Madam'. A Jack placed on the pile is asked, 'How do you do, Sir?'. If an Ace is laid it must be covered by the palm of the hand. The first player to do any of these things wins all the cards on the pile. The game ends when somebody has all the cards, leaving their opponents empty-handed. Remember, the greeting must be word perfect or the player has to give a card to each of the other players.

BLACKJACK
Two or more players
Two dice, counters and a pot

The object of this game is to score twenty-one points, or to be the closest player to twenty-one. If a score exceeds twenty-one the player is out of the game. Everyone puts in the same number of counters to form the bank. Each player has only one turn per game but during that turn he or she may throw the dice any number of times. When the score gets to fourteen the player may choose to throw just one die. The skill in this game is knowing when to stop. If the score is seventeen, for example, the player has to be very careful. It may be wiser to stop as one more throw could put the score over twenty-one. If there is a tie the dice are thrown again. It is a good idea to decide before you start how many rounds you will play. At the end of every round the winner takes the bank. The player with the most counters at the end of all the rounds is the overall winner. Of course, if you run out of counters, the game will stop anyway.

GO BOOM
Two or more players

In this game Aces are high. The object is to get rid of all the cards. Each player has seven cards each and the others are stacked in the middle. The first player leads with any card. Each player must follow with a card of the same suit. If the player cannot, he or she has to pick up a card from the central pile. The player with the highest card wins the trick and starts the next hand. When someone has got rid of all his or her cards he or she cries out, 'Boom'.

RED AND BLACK
Two players
This is a very good game for travelling as it requires no dealing. One player holds the pack. He or she holds each card up in turn so that the other player can only see the back. The guesser then has to say whether the card is black or red. if he or she is right, the guesser collects the card, but if he or she is wrong it stays in the pack. Once the pack has been gone through once each player should have a pile of cards. The guesser then puts down a card, face up. The other player puts a card beside it. If they match in value the matcher collects all the cards. The game is over when one player has all the cards.

OLD MAID
Two or more players
The object of the game is to avoid being the Old Maid. First of all a Queen is removed from the pack. The rest of the cards are shuffled and distributed between the players. Each player sorts these cards into pairs. The person who dealt then holds up his cards to the next player, who chooses one. If this gives her a pair, she places it face down and takes another card. If it does not make a pair she offers her cards to the next player. This goes on until all the cards are paired. The player who is left with one Queen is the Old Maid.

If there are only two players they will need quite big hands as there are a lot of cards to hold!

HOLD YOUR HORSES
Two or more players

All the cards are dealt out between the players. Each card has a value from one to thirteen. Ace counts as one and the king is thirteen. Each player in turn puts down a card face down on the pile calling 'Number one, number two' etc. as they go. At any time another player may challenge them and call, 'Hold your Horses'. If the player has truly laid the number which was called out the challenger must pick up all the cards. If the player has not laid the correct number he or she must pick up all the cards. The game restarts with number one. The winner is the first player to get rid of all his cards.

SNIP SNAP SNORUM
Three players

If anyone is sitting near your group when you play this game they may think that you are rather an odd crowd! First of all the cards are dealt out between the players. The first player puts down a card. The next must lay a card of the same value but in a different suit. For example, if the first player lays the three of Clubs the next player might lay the three of Hearts. As he does this the player says 'Snip'. If the next player can lay another three, say the three of Spades, she puts it down saying 'Snap'. The last three to be put down is 'Snorum'. If a player is unable to put down a card he or she must say 'Pass'. The winner of each hand is the player who says 'Snorum'. This player then begins the next round. The object is to get rid of all your cards.

WIN HIGH
Two players

The cards are dealt equally between two players. Each player piles his cards, face down in front of him. Both players turn over the top of their pile to start another pile by the first. The player with the highest card takes both cards and adds them to the bottom of his pack. If both turned-up cards happen to be the same the next card is turned over until one is higher. The winner then takes all the cards. The game ends when one player has collected all the cards.

CATCH THE JACK
Two players

All the cards are dealt equally between the two players. Each player turns over a card in turn, one on top of the other. If someone plays a Jack the players must put their hands, palm down, over it. The one who puts his or her palm down first picks up the pile of cards. The winner is the first player to win all the cards. If someone puts their hand on a card that is not a Jack the card must be handed over to the opponent.

Do make sure that you use the opposite hand to cover the card to the one that turns the card over.

SOLO SNAP

This is a game to play by yourself. Shuffle the cards and then begin to deal the cards, face upwards, one on top of the other. As you deal you call out a sequence of numbers . . . Ace/one, two, three, etc. and ending with Jack, Queen, King. Whenever your call and the card you are dealing are the same, you put it to one side. When you get to the end of the pack, shuffle the remaining cards and start again. Do this six times only. Record your score by counting the cards that you have left. The object is to lower your score each time.

It is also possible to play this game with two players, if you have two packs of cards. The player with the least number of cards at the end would be the winner.

SPEED SNAP
If you find ordinary snap a little tame, this version may be more to your liking. Instead of laying down cards onto one pile both players put down cards at the same time on adjacent piles. You really have to concentrate hard as the game is very fast.

INDOOR GOLF
Two or more players
This is a way of playing golf without setting foot outside. All you need are three dice. The first player throws the dice. If all the numbers are different this represents one 'stroke'. The player keeps throwing until he or she scores a double. When each player has had a turn the one who scored a double with the fewest 'strokes' wins the 'hole'. As on a golf course there are eighteen holes to win. The player who wins the most wins the game.